earrings

by Tansy Wilson

THE GUILD OF MASTER CRAFTSMAN

PUBLICATIONS

GUILD OF
MASTER CRAFTSMAN
PUBLICATIONS

First published 2011 by
Guild of Master Craftsman Publications Ltd
Castle Place, 166 High Street, Lewes,
East Sussex BN7 1XU

ISBN 978 1 86108 876 5

A catalogue record for this book is available from
the British Library.

Set in King and Myriad
Colour origination by GMC
Reprographics
Printed and bound in China by
Hing Yip

Publisher Jonathan Bailey
Production Manager Jim Bulley
Managing Editor Gerrie Purcell
Editor Judith Chamberlain-Webber
Managing Art Editor Gilda Pacitti
Art Editor Rebecca Mothersole
Photographers Andrew Perris and
Rebecca Mothersole
Designer Sarah Howerd

contents

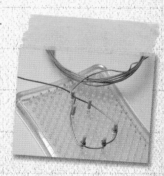

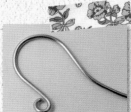

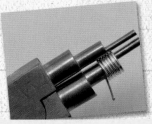

SPIRALS

WRITING

SHAPES

CHAIN MAIL

CHERRIES

CLUSTERS

RETRO

DROPLETS

The Projects

BUTTONS

SHOES

FEATHERS

SHELLS

TREATS

SEASIDE

SECRET

VICTORIANA

VENICE

AUTUMN

CHILLIES

SWEETS

Tools and equipment

THE FOLLOWING PAGES LIST AND EXPLAIN SOME OF THE MOST COMMONLY USED TOOLS YOU WILL NEED TO MAKE YOUR EARRINGS.

pliers

When holding, forming or shaping pieces of jewellery, the most common tools used are pliers. You can get different types that are designed for particular uses. However, even if you have just one pair of pliers, you should be able to tackle most jobs.

Round-nose pliers

These pliers have totally round tapered jaws that start small at the very tip and increase to a larger circumference at the base. They are used for making eyepins, wrapping loops and shaping wire in general.

Flat-nose pliers

These pliers have flat parallel jaws top and bottom. They are very handy for bending sharp corners or straightening wire, crimping flat ribbon crimps and holding, opening or closing jumprings and other small components.

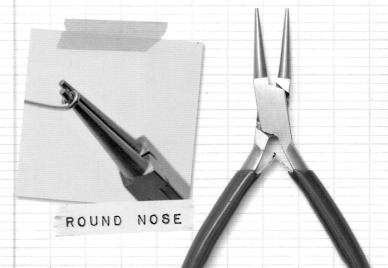

ROUND NOSE

FLAT NOSE

Snipe-nose pliers

Sometimes known as chain-nose pliers, these pliers have half round jaws with flat parallel inside faces that touch. They are also tapered from small at the very tip of the nose to a larger half round at the base. Their unique shape makes them ideal for holding small jewellery components, opening and closing chain links or jumprings and shaping wire in general.

Multi-sized looping pliers

With many sizes of round jaws on one surface, these pliers allow you to make jumprings and loops to a certain size. Wire wrap mandrels are a less expensive version of exactly the same tool.

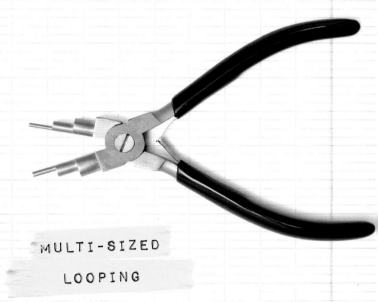

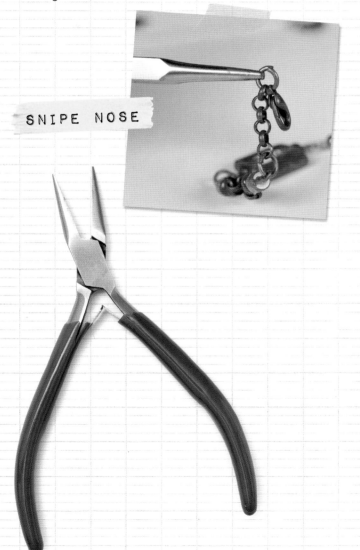

SNIPE NOSE

MULTI-SIZED

LOOPING

Tools and equipment

cutters

There are various types and sizes of cutters used in jewellery making. To simplify their uses, top and side cutters are used for cutting thin materials and wire. Snips are used for cutting sheet material while piercing saws cut wire, tube or sheet metal.

Top cutters

The actual cutting surface on this tool is at the very top, as the name suggests. Materials such as wire can be cut at 90 degrees, extremely close and flush to your piece.

Side cutters

These work in a very similar way to top cutters; however, this time the cutting surface is on the side of the tool. The nose is also slightly tapered to gain access to smaller areas in your piece.

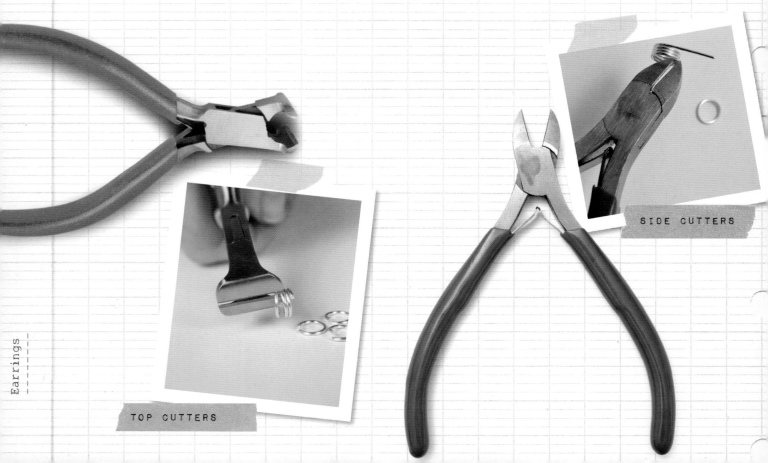

TOP CUTTERS

SIDE CUTTERS

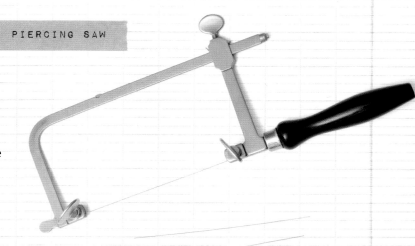

Snips

Snips are often seen as a pair of scissors for sheet metal. They are also useful for trimming ribbon or leather. Be careful, however, as they can leave a mark on the surface when cutting.

Piercing saw and blades

This tool uses separate saw blades for cutting wire, tube or sheet metal. It gives an extremely clean cut without marking the surface at all. Piercing saws are ideal for making jumprings, as they cut the wire completely flush without leaving an indent. This ensures that the jumprings close nice and tight.

SNIPS

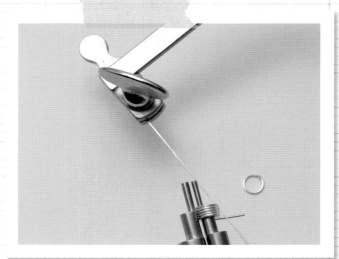

Tools and equipment

miscellaneous tools

Bradawl

With its very sharp point, a bradawl is a very useful tool for piercing a hole in various plastics and fabrics. It is not recommended for metal sheet or wire.

Bead mat

This is a less expensive equivalent to the bead board (see opposite) without the compartments. Essentially, it is just a cushioned soft mat that stops your beads and findings from rolling around.

BRADAWL

BEAD MAT

Thing-a-ma-jig

This tool has pins or pegs that you can place in any combination into the jig base to make elaborate loops, chandelier components or simply unusual shapes in wire. It is very useful as it's easy to replicate your design consistently. You can also make your own (see page 25).

THING-A-MA-JIG

Bead board

This is not an essential tool, but it is very useful to have when working with several beads. The channels on the board stop the beads from rolling around while compartments in the middle allow you to place the findings you will be using for that particular piece.

Emery sticks and papers

These sanding and polishing sticks are very beneficial for softening sharp edges on wire or sheet metal, especially when making ear hooks and hoops.

EMERY STICK

BEAD BOARD

Tape measure

A tape measure is an essential tool for measuring your materials so you can keep a record of how much you have used but also for ensuring you make the other earring the same size!

Adhesive

Adhesive, such as superglue, is ideal for use on all types of beads and threads. It is quick-setting even on absorbent surfaces, and is particularly handy for adding a drop onto knots for extra security.

ADHESIVE

TAPE MEASURE

Tools and equipment

Materials

beads

There is such a massive variety of beads available that it can be daunting to know which ones to buy. Perhaps start by purchasing beads in your favourite colours and shapes and keep adding to your collection as you go. Remember that beads and charms don't necessarily have to match!

Earrings

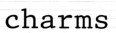

charms

From handmade polymer clay or lampwork glass through to cast metal shapes, there is an increasing number of gorgeous fun and funky charms available. They are a great way of adding colour and character to your designs. Where possible, look for charms with detail on both the front and back, so it doesn't matter if they spin round on the earring.

recycled pieces

You don't always have to buy new beads and charms for your earrings. Keep hold of any broken jewellery, watch pieces or buttons from your favourite old clothes and re-use them in your designs. Charity shops or jumble sales are often great places for finding unique pieces and vintage beads at bargain prices. Also keep a look out for left-over ribbon, beautiful feathers lying on the ground or even shells from the beach.

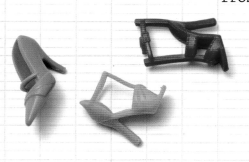

findings

Findings is a word given to all the little bits and pieces that are not beads or charms used in jewellery making. There is a huge choice available to buy that are already made for you. On these pages are the ones I regularly use throughout this book; some of these you can make yourself, too. Have a look in the basic techniques section starting on page 18.

open earring hooks

Open earring hooks with a ball are decorative earring hooks that hang from your ear. They have an open loop at the bottom from which you can hang beads or chain.

jumprings

A jumpring is a single ring of metal that is mainly used to join or link pieces together. You close the ring to secure the item into place.

ribbon crimps

These little metal crimps are used for holding together materials like ribbon, leather thong or feathers. They often have a loop attached so you can easily connect them to other findings.

flat back stud fittings with scroll

This type of stud earring pushes through the ear, but instead of a loop to hang beads from, you glue your beads directly onto the flat surface.

plain earring hooks

These are a plainer version of the decorative earring hooks with a ball. This type for is best suited for more simple ideas. That's for you to decide!

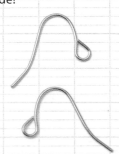

stud fittings with open loop & scroll

This type of earring has a straight post that is pushed through your ear; it is secured at the back by a scroll which is also known as a butterfly. It has a loop at the bottom from which you can hang beads or chain.

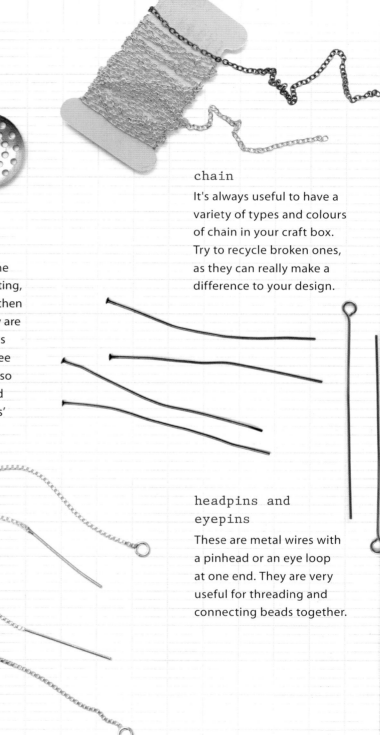

sieves

These are small metal discs that have holes in. You literally sew beads onto them to create beaded circles of colour. Have a look at the 'Retro' project (see page 56).

chandeliers

These are a connector, usually hanging from the earring hook or stud fitting, from which you would then hang many beads. They are often very decorative, as shown in 'Victoriana' (see page 96) but you can also buy plain hoops as used in the alternative 'Shoes' project (see page 70).

chain

It's always useful to have a variety of types and colours of chain in your craft box. Try to recycle broken ones, as they can really make a difference to your design.

headpins and eyepins

These are metal wires with a pinhead or an eye loop at one end. They are very useful for threading and connecting beads together.

ear threads

These are fine chains that thread directly through your ear and simply dangle at a similar length at the front and back.

Basic techniques

The following pages illustrate some of the basic skills you will find useful when making your own earrings. Obviously, you can purchase pre-made fittings like jumprings, earring wire hooks or eyepins; however, sometimes you may need something of a particular size or design that is difficult to source.

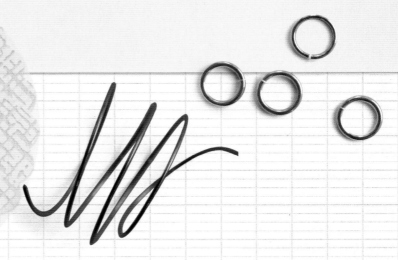

WORKING WITH WIRE

MASTERING BASIC TECHNIQUES IN MANIPULATING WIRE IS FUNDAMENTAL FOR ALL YOUR PROJECTS, FROM MAKING SIMPLE JUMPRINGS AND EARRING WIRES TO MORE COMPLICATED CHANDELIER PIECES. MAKING YOUR OWN COMPONENTS RATHER THAN BUYING READY-MADE PIECES WILL BOOST YOUR CONFIDENCE AND EXPAND YOUR DESIGNS.

One of the main considerations when using wire is planning. Ensure that your work is well thought out before you start. Also, keep your wire on the roll where possible, cutting it off only at the last minute. You will not always know how much wire is needed.

jumprings

A jumpring is a single ring of metal that is mainly used to join or link pieces together. You close the ring to secure the item into place.

Opening and closing jumprings

1 Hold a pair of pliers with a flat parallel nose in each hand so they are facing each other.

2 With the opening of the jumpring at the top, grip one half of the ring with the pliers in your left hand and the other half with the pliers in your right.

3 Twist the left-hand pliers away from your body and the right-hand pliers towards your body. This will open the jumpring without losing the circle shape.

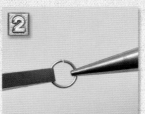

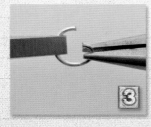

MAKING JUMPRINGS

1 Tightly coil a length of round wire around a wire wrap mandrel or multi-sized looping pliers. If you do not have either of these tools, wrap the wire around an available cylindrical shape, for example, a pen or a lipstick case (depending on the size of jumpring required). The number of coils made will determine the number of jumprings you will make.

2 Slide the coil of wire up until one loop of wire comes off the tool or cylindrical object used.

3 Using a piercing saw to create a straight edge, cut through the first coil, then push the second coil off the former and cut through this ring. Continue this process cutting off one ring at a time.

4 If you don't have a piercing saw, use side cutters or top cutters to cut the jumprings off one at a time.

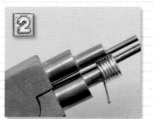

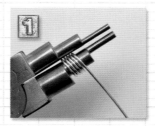

Basic techniques

earring hoops

An ideal gauge of wire to use for making your own hoops is $^1/_{32}$in (0.8mm) or $^3/_{64}$in (1mm). The beauty of making your own is that you can have whatever size you want. Once made, this style of earring also allows you to easily thread on beads or charms without necessarily having to use any other findings.

MAKING EARRING HOOPS

1 Coil round wire twice around a cylindrical former, such as a marker pen. The size of the former will determine how large the hoop will be. An average size is approximately $^{25}/_{32}$in (20mm).

2 Cut through the coils to create two separate hoops of the same size.

3 With round-nose pliers, grip the very end of the wire on one of the hoops and turn it to form a small closed loop.

4 Hold the other end of the wire with flat parallel nose pliers and bend it approximately 45 degrees so that it fits through the loop. Once you have fastened the hoop, you may need to tweak the shape of the hoop with your fingers to make it round again.

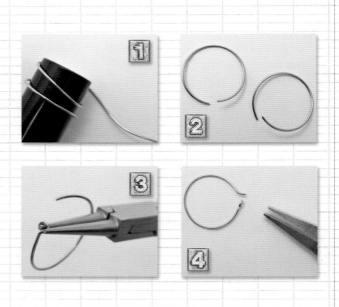

earring hooks

You can buy a wide variety of pre-made earring hooks, but it is very useful knowing how to make your own so you can make your designs truly unique. Once you have grasped this basic technique, you can experiment with trying to make different sizes or using other colours of wire. Again, an ideal gauge of wire to use is $\frac{1}{32}$in (0.8mm) or $\frac{3}{64}$in (1mm).

MAKING EARRING HOOKS

1 Cut approximately 2in (50mm) of round wire and grip the very end of the wire with round-nose pliers.

2 Turn the pliers to form a small closed loop.

3 Bend the other end of the wire around a cylindrical former approximately $\frac{3}{8}$in (10mm) in diameter, such as a pen. The larger the former, the larger the loop. This forms the hook that goes through your ear.

4 Gently bend the remaining straight piece of wire coming out of the loop away from the former and over your finger. Trim the excess wire if necessary.

5 If the end of the hook is sharp, file it down using an emery stick or emery paper.

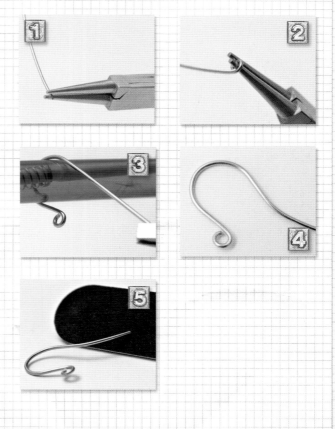

eyepins and headpins

The difference between an eyepin and a headpin is that a headpin is a length of wire with a little pinhead at one end. This allows you to thread beads onto the wire without them falling off. An eyepin is also a length of wire, but this has a loop at one end. This also allows you to thread beads on the wire without them falling off but, more importantly, allows you to add onto the loop as well. An average gauge of wire to use when making eyepins is $\frac{1}{32}$in (0.8mm) but remember, if you are using small beads you may need to use a thinner wire!

MAKING EYEPINS

1 Using round-nose pliers, hold a piece of wire at the very end. The length of wire is determined by how many beads you want to thread on.

2 Turn the pliers to form a small closed loop.

3 Move this loop in the pliers so the long end can be pushed against the other round-nose jaw to centre the eyepin loop over the remaining wire. How far up the nose of the pliers you grip the wire will determine the size of the eye hole.

open eye loops

An open eye loop is a loop you make as close to the top of a bead as possible. This loop will allow you to link your bead onto other components such as an earring hook or chain.

MAKING OPEN EYE LOOPS AT THE TOP OF A BEAD

1 Thread a headpin through your chosen bead.

2 Bend the long length of the headpin back against the bead.

3 Using round-nose pliers, grip the wire at the very top of the bead. Holding the long end of the wire, wrap this all the way around the nose of the pliers until the two ends of wire meet up.

4 With side or top cutters, cut the wire at the point where the two wires meet.

5 Holding the very end of the cut wire in round-nose pliers, bend the wire in tightly to form a perfectly shaped eye hole.

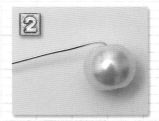
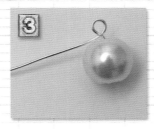

closed loops

Closed loops have a very similar purpose to open eye loops except once you have wired your chosen bead on to your design, the only way to remove it would be to physically cut it off. Using closed loops is the most secure method of linking beads.

WIRING ON A BEAD USING A CLOSED LOOP

1 Thread a headpin through your chosen bead.

2 Bend the long length of the headpin back against the bead.

3 Use round-nose pliers to grip the wire at the very top of the bead. Bend the long length of the headpin around the nose of the pliers, nearly meeting the wire you are holding in your pliers. This should form a hook shape.

4 Thread the wire onto a component, such as a chain or chandelier fitting, so that it hangs down from the hook created in step 3.

5 Hold the top of the hook with snipe nose pliers. In your other hand, hold the long end of the headpin and start to wrap it around the hook, spiralling the wire around itself.

6 Continue to spiral the wire around until it forms a spiral on top of the chosen bead. Using side or top cutters, cut off any excess wire as close to the spiral as possible.

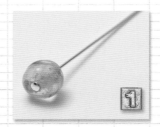

chandeliers

Chandeliers can be any size or shape and they usually contain a number of loops from which you can hang beads, chain or charms.

MAKING A CHANDELIER FITTING

1 Using a thing-a-ma-jig, place pins in a simple pattern. You could also use a piece of wood with some nails hammered in. Remember to cut the tops of the nails off afterwards, so that the wire slides off easily.

2 Keeping the wire on the roll, use wire about $1/32$in (0.8mm) or $3/64$in (1mm) thick, as this holds its shape better.

3 Leave a long length of wire at the start of the first or top pin. This will make eye loops when you have taken the wire off the former.

4 Begin to wrap the wire around the pins and create loops at the bottom of your design. Keep the wire taut until you get back to where you started.

5 Cut the wire off the roll, ensuring you leave another long length for making eye loops or for wrapping around the other end.

6 To make an attachment to fix the chandelier onto an earring hook, make an eye loop at one end of the wire as close to the top of your design as possible. Cut away any excess wire.

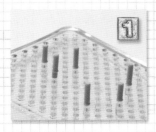

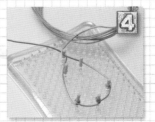

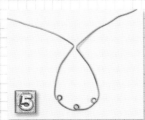
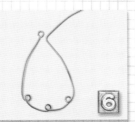

7 Wrap the other long end of your wire around the base of the eye loop, spiralling the wire around itself to make a neat coil. Again, cut away any excess wire.

beaded balls

Knowing how to make a simple beaded ball is a great asset for giving any earring individuality. This is easily achieved by choosing beads from a multitude of colours, shapes and sizes and varying the way you mix these elements together.

MAKING BEADED BALLS

1 Take approximately 9¾in (25cm) of ¹⁄₈₀in (0.3mm) thick wire or nylon and thread three beads onto it.

2 Centre the beads on the wire, then add another bead onto the left-hand end.

3 Thread the right-hand end of the wire through the most recently added bead, going the opposite way.

4 Pull the two ends together so the four beads are clustered together in a circle at the centre of the wire.

5 Add another bead to both ends of the wire, pushing them close to the circle of beads created in step 4.

6 Thread another bead onto the left-hand end. Pass the right-hand end of the wire through this bead in the opposite direction. Pull the wire until you have two circles of beads.

7 Repeat steps 5–6 to create three circles of beads.

8 Add one more bead onto both ends of the wire and push these along to join the others.

9 Pass the left-hand end through the very first bead at the tip of the first circle. Pass the right-hand end through the same bead but in the opposite direction.

10 Pull these ends so that the beads will curl together and form a ball.

11 To secure the wires, thread one end through the circle of beads until it comes round to meet the other end.

12 Tie both threads together and add a small drop of glue if necessary to secure. Cut away excess thread.

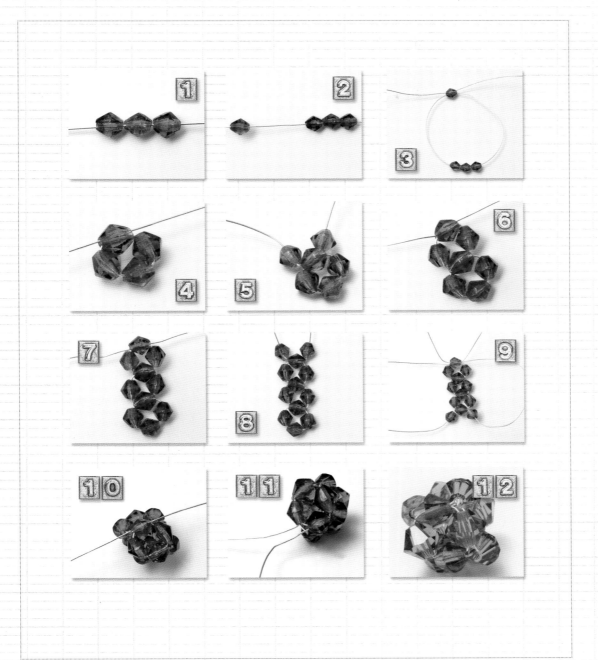

wire

spirals

This simple but effective design will give you the confidence to start using wire and creating your own shapes!

Everything you will need...

The simplicity of this design is a good starting point. It shows off the wire-wrapped details, and there is always something satisfying about a spiral.

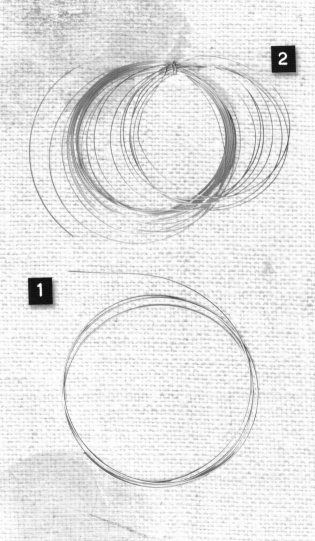

1 $^{3}/_{64}$in (1mm) silver wire

2 $^{1}/_{48}$in (0.6mm) silver wire

round-nose pliers

snipe-nose pliers

side cutters

Assembling spirals

1 Make an earring hoop of your chosen size (see basic techniques on page 20).

2 Cut off 8in (20cm) of $^3/_{64}$in (1mm) wire using side cutters. Holding the very end of the wire with round-nose pliers, create a loop large enough for $^3/_{64}$in (1mm) wire to pass through.

3 Hold the loop with snipe-nose pliers and start to spiral the wire around itself, turning the spiral each time to keep it even.

4 When you have created three spirals, take hold of the other end of the wire at the very tip and bend it back on

itself to make a small kink. Squash this kink as tightly as possible, then, holding it flat, start to spiral the wire the other way around the kink. Continue spiralling until you meet the other spiral.

5 Thread the spiral design onto the hoop through the hole in the centre of the smaller spiral, keeping the hoop open.

6 Cut off 4in (10cm) of $^1/_{48}$in (0.6mm) wire. Hold the wire against part of the hoop, then start to wrap it around the hoop, keeping the wire as tight and even as possible. Keep a count

of how many times you wrap it round, so that you can match it on the other side.

7 Use side cutters to cut away the excess wire. If necessary, use snipe-nose pliers to squash the wire coil tightly against the hoop.

8 Repeat steps 6–7 to wrap wire around the other side of the earring hoop. Finally, repeat the process to create the other earring.

EXPERIMENT WITH DIFFERENT THICKNESSES OF WIRE.

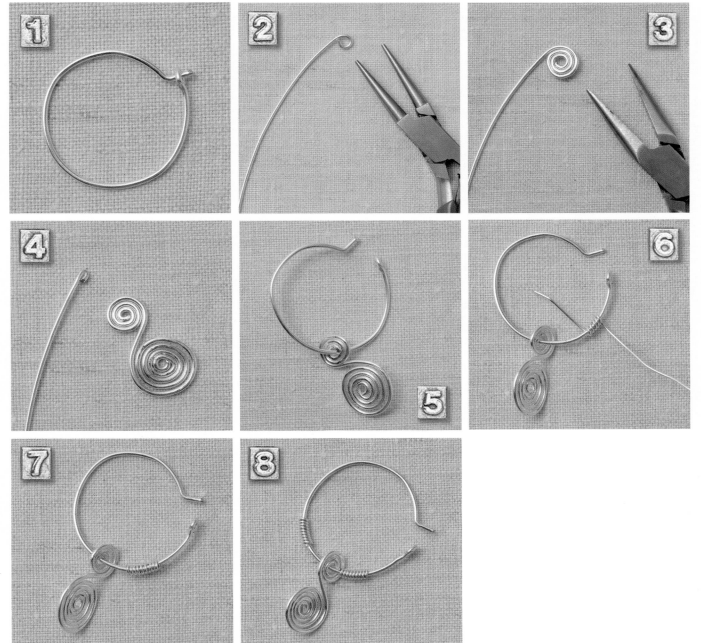

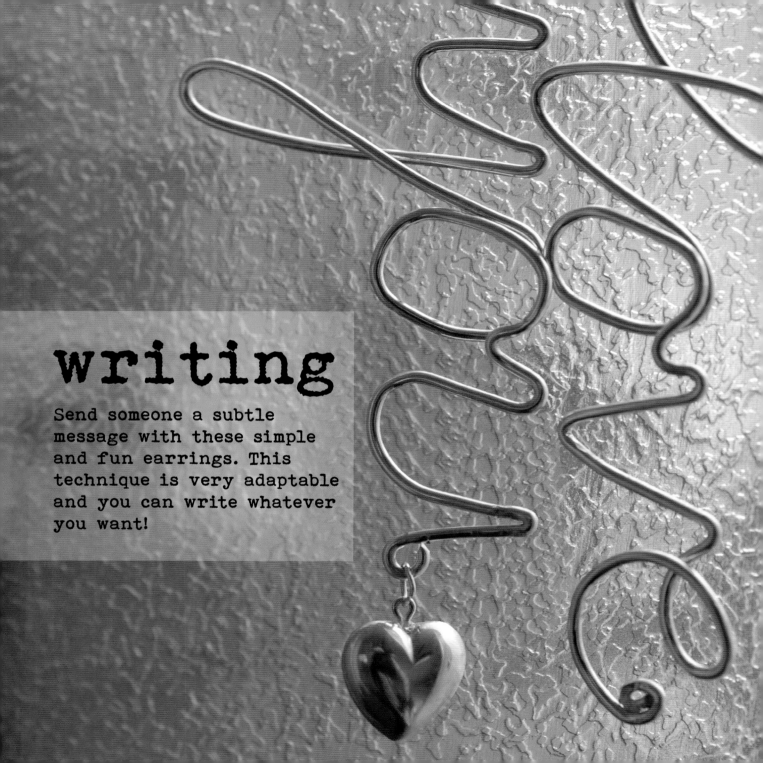

writing

Send someone a subtle
message with these simple
and fun earrings. This
technique is very adaptable
and you can write whatever
you want!

Everything you will need...

One of the main considerations with using wire is planning. Keep your wire on the roll – where possible cutting it off only at the last minute. You will not always know how much wire a word is going to take!

1. A silver heart charm
2. 2 silver plain open earring wires
3. $^1/_{16}$in (1.2mm) silver wire
4. 1 x $^1/_8$in (3mm) silver jumpring

   round-nose pliers

   side cutters

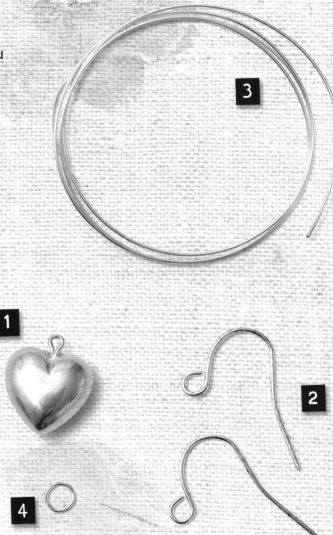

Assembling writing

1 Decide on the words you are going to use, then draw them to scale on a piece of paper to create a template.

2 Keeping the silver wire on the roll, use round-nose pliers to make a small loop at the very end of the wire.

3 Start your writing from this loop. You may find it easier to bend the wire with your fingers rather than use pliers all the time. Continue to follow your template with the wire until your word is finished.

4 If you wish to hang a charm off the end of your word, ensure you finish the last letter with a small loop and, using a $1/8$in (3mm) jumpring, attach your charm.

5 Open the loop on an earring hook, then thread it onto the small loop of your word and close.

6 Finally, repeat the process to create the other earring.

The letters should all be joined up and their tops and tails evenly balanced so that the word hangs straight.

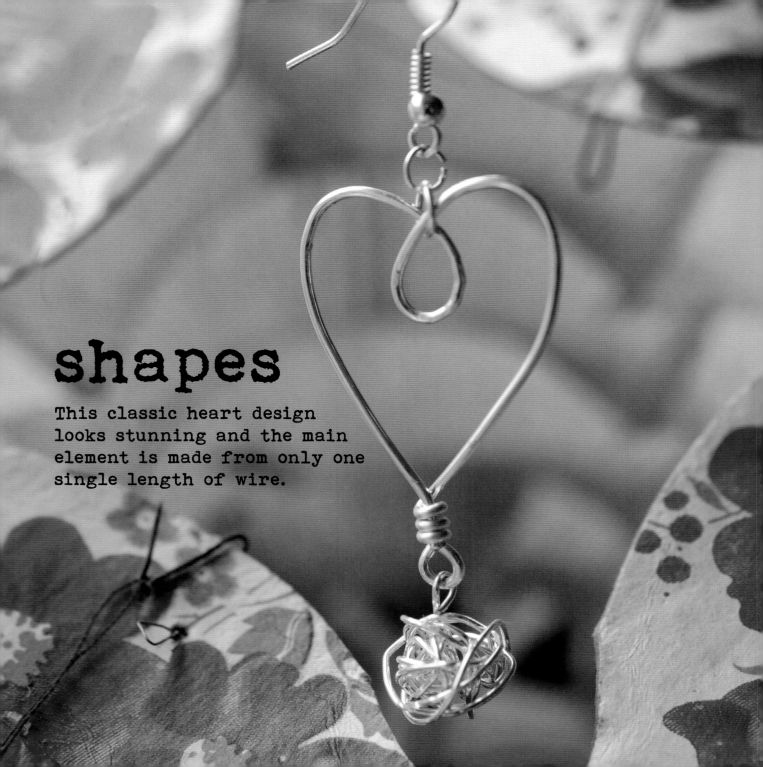

shapes

This classic heart design
looks stunning and the main
element is made from only one
single length of wire.

Everything you will need...

This classic heart design looks equally as attractive left simple or with an additional bead for a splash of colour and sparkle.

×2

1. $^3/_{64}$ (1mm) silver wire (approx 8in/20cm per earring)
2. 2 x $^3/_{16}$in (5mm) silver jumprings
3. 2 x $^1/_8$in (3mm) silver jumprings
4. 2 silver earring hooks with ball
5. $^1/_{48}$in (0.6mm) wire

   flat-nose pliers

   round-nose pliers

   side cutters

Variation:

6. $^1/_{80}$in (0.3mm) silver wire
7. 24 x $^5/_{32}$in (4mm) crystals or beads
8. 2 beads (optional)

shapes

Assembling shapes

1 Cut off 8in (20cm) of ³/₆₄in (1mm) wire. Form a loose loop roughly in the centre of the wire. For the variation, add a bead to settle in the middle of this loop.

2 Holding both ends of the wire, bend them round symmetrically to form a heart shape.

3 Using flat-nose pliers, make one end of the wire straight where the two wires cross at the bottom of the heart.

4 Spiral the other end of the wire around the straight end of the wire a couple of times. Cut away any excess using side cutters.

5 With the remaining length of straight wire, form an eye loop and again cut away any excess wire.

6 Open a ³/₁₆in (5mm) jumpring and link this to the top of the heart and to a ¹/₈in (3mm) jumpring, then close.

7 Open the loop on an earring wire, link the ¹/₈in (3mm) jumpring to it and close.

8 Make wire balls by scrunching a length of wire and continue to keep wrapping the wire around itself until it is approximately ³/₈in (10mm) in diameter. Leave a length of wire long enough to make an eye loop at the top of your wire ball bead. Attach the wire ball to the loop at the bottom of the heart.

9 Finally, repeat the process to create the other earring. For the variation, make your own beaded balls (see basic techniques page 26).

WHEN MAKING BEADED BALLS, BE SURE TO LEAVE A PIECE OF WIRE OR NYLON AT ONE END THAT IS LONG ENOUGH TO TURN INTO AN EYE LOOP.

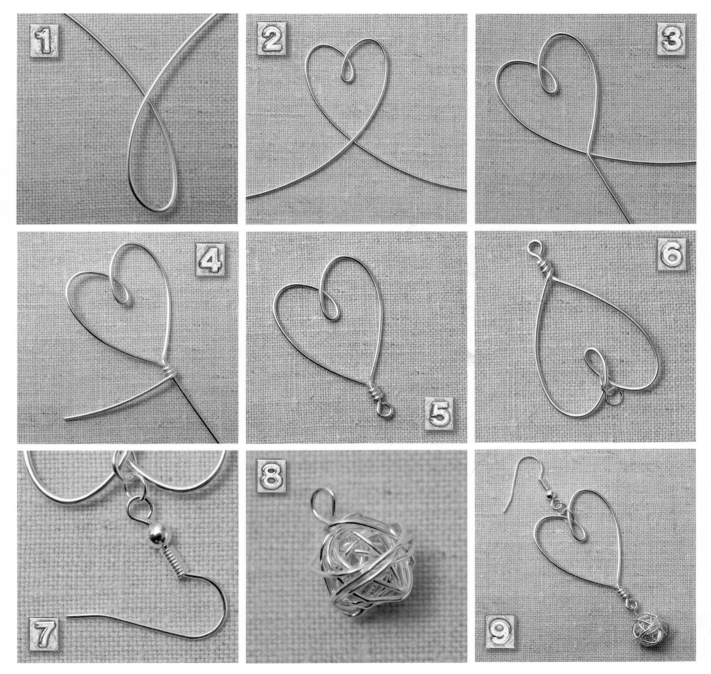

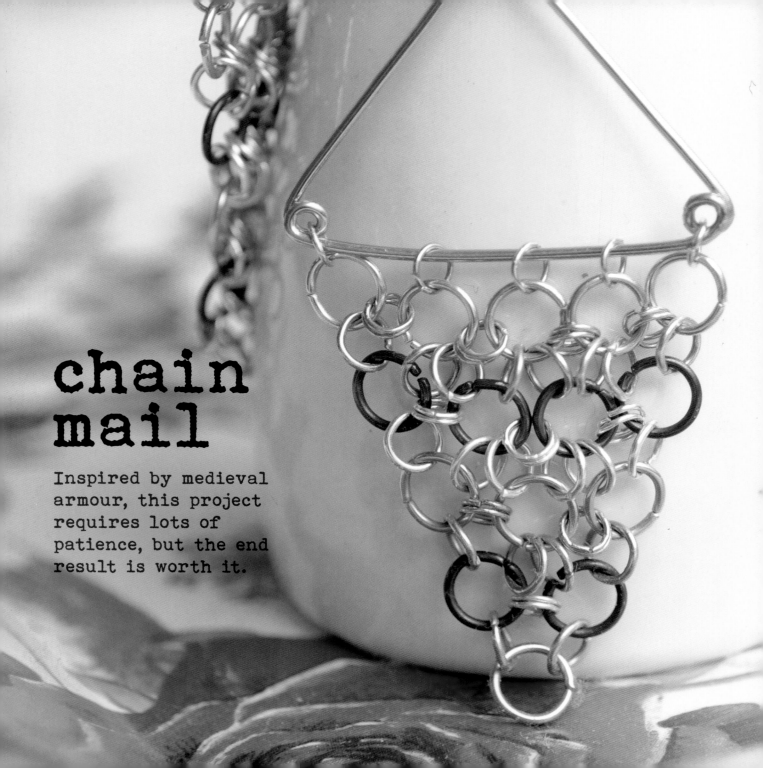

chain
mail

Inspired by medieval
armour, this project
requires lots of
patience, but the end
result is worth it.

Everything you will need...

Making lots of jumprings in different thicknesses of wire, sizes and colours can create a lot of fun variations on this simple design.

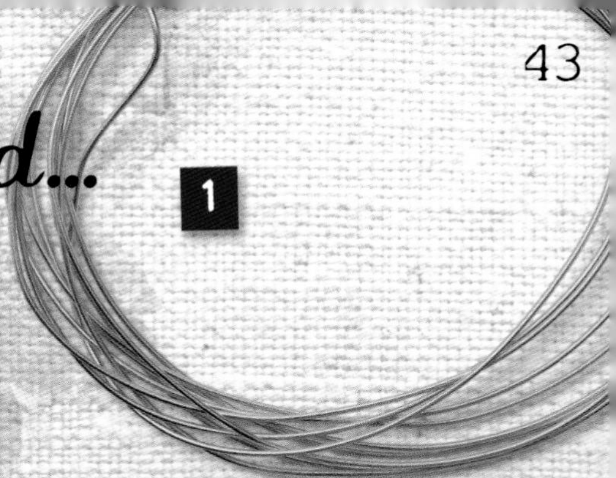

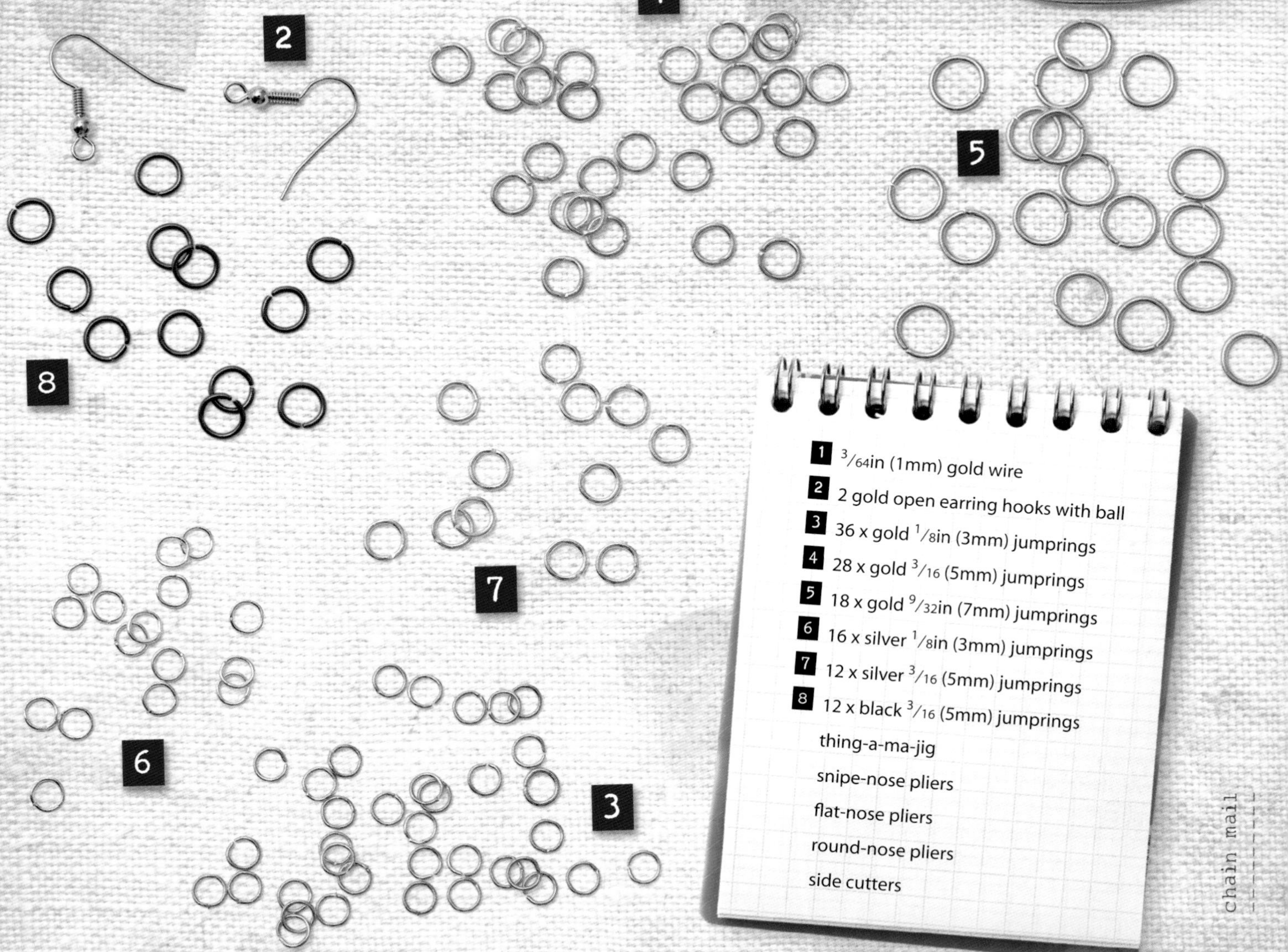

1 $^3/_{64}$in (1mm) gold wire
2 2 gold open earring hooks with ball
3 36 x gold $^1/_8$in (3mm) jumprings
4 28 x gold $^3/_{16}$ (5mm) jumprings
5 18 x gold $^9/_{32}$in (7mm) jumprings
6 16 x silver $^1/_8$in (3mm) jumprings
7 12 x silver $^3/_{16}$ (5mm) jumprings
8 12 x black $^3/_{16}$ (5mm) jumprings

thing-a-ma-jig

snipe-nose pliers

flat-nose pliers

round-nose pliers

side cutters

chain mail

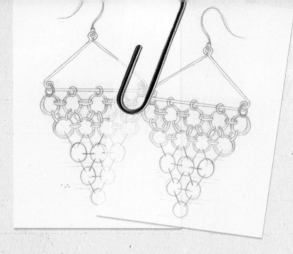

Assembling chain mail

1 If you have a thing-a-ma-jig, place three guide pins 1 1/8in (30mm) apart to form an equilateral triangle. Alternatively, hammer three nails into a piece of wood to use as a template (see basic techniques on page 25). Leaving an end of about 2in (5cm) and keeping the wire on the roll, wrap the 3/64in (1mm) wire around one of the pins to make a small loop. Carry the wire onto the next pin and wrap it around to make another small loop.

2 Bend both ends of the wire up to the third pin and make kinks in them where they meet the pin. Cut the wire off approximately 1in (2cm) from the kink.

3 Remove the shape from your template. Where you made the two kinks in either ends of the wire, form two small forward-facing eye loops. Cut away any excess wire. If necessary, use flat-nose pliers to make sure the eye loops line up flush together.

4 Open a 3/16in (5mm) jumpring and link both eye loops together. Use the same jumpring to attach the chandelier to the loop on the earring hook and close.

5 Open 5 x 1/8in (3mm) gold jumprings. Put one in each loop at the end of the chandelier and the remaining three on the straight bar, then close.

6 Open 5 x 9/32in (7mm) gold jumprings, loop one onto each of the 1/8in (3mm) jumprings and close.

7 Open 2 x 1/8in (3mm) jumprings and link one of the 9/32in (7mm) jumprings to the next 9/32in (7mm) jumpring. Repeat this step until all the 9/32in (7mm) jumprings are linked by 2 x 1/8in (3mm) jumprings.

8 Using 4 x 9/32in (7mm) black jumprings, link 2 x 1/8in (3mm) silver jumprings between each so you link all the black jumprings together. Then place them on the table. Repeat this process, this time using 3 x 9/32in (7mm) gold jumprings and 4 x 1/8in (3mm) gold jumprings. Repeat the next row using 2 x 9/32in (7mm) black jumprings and 2 x 1/8in (3mm) silver jumprings finally linking 1 x 9/32in (7mm) gold jumpring to the very bottom of the 2 x 9/32 (7mm) black jumprings using 2 x 3/16in (5mm) jumprings. Lay all the rows on the table.

9 Link the rows shown in step 8 by using the 3/16in (5mm) jumprings. Link your four rows to the very first row you put onto the chandelier. Repeat the process to create the other earring.

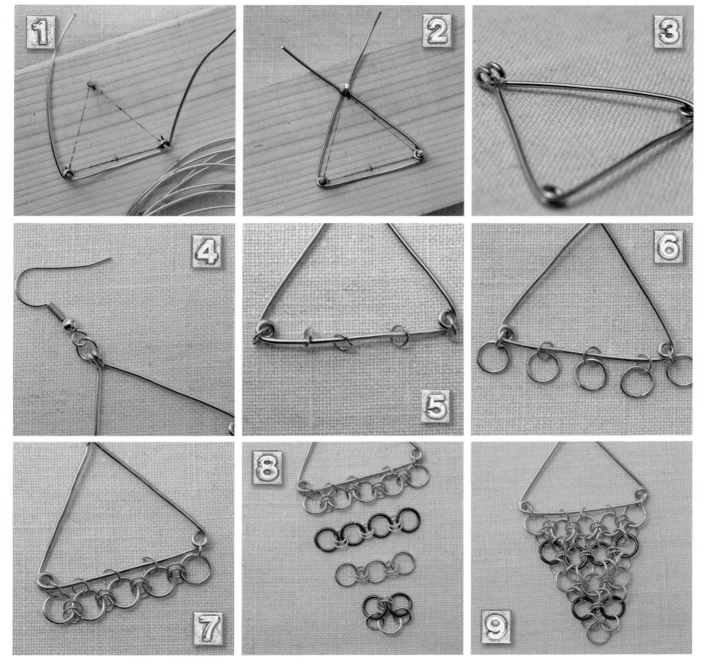

beads

cherries

Cherries not only taste great, but their iconic image is used for numerous artistic projects. This design can be your own take on this pretty fruit.

Everything you will need...

Threading red glass beads onto wire and spiralling them up into a tight circle instantly creates that glossy cherry look.

1 2 copper plain open earring hooks

2 2 x 1/8in (3mm) copper jumprings

3 2 leaf charms

4 60 red glass beads

5 1/32in (0.71mm) coloured copper craft wire (mid-brown)

side cutters

snipe nose pliers

Assembling cherries

1 Cut 8in (20cm) of the $1/32$in (0.71mm) copper craft wire and thread a red glass bead onto it.

2 Wrap the wire back around the bead and twist around the longer length of wire to ensure that the bead is secured. Cut off excess wire with side cutters.

3 Thread another 29 of the beads onto the wire.

4 Holding all the beads so that they line up tightly together, start to spiral the beads on the wire to form a large flat round shape.

5 When the beads are tightly spiralled, pass the long end of the wire directly under the row below, then bend it back up to secure the spiral.

6 Make a small loop in the long end of the wire about 2in (50mm) up from the cherry. Wrap the wire around the 'stalk' to close the loop. Cut off any excess wire if necessary.

7 Open the loop on an earring hook and thread the completed cherry onto it and close.

8 Open a $1/8$in (3mm) jumpring and thread the leaf charm on to it. Link the jumpring to the loop at the top of the cherry, then close.

9 Finally, repeat the process to create the other earring.

I USED THESE ENAMELLED LEAVES, BUT YOU COULD USE GREEN GLASS BEADS ON A WIRE TO MAKE YOUR OWN INDIVIDUAL PIECES.

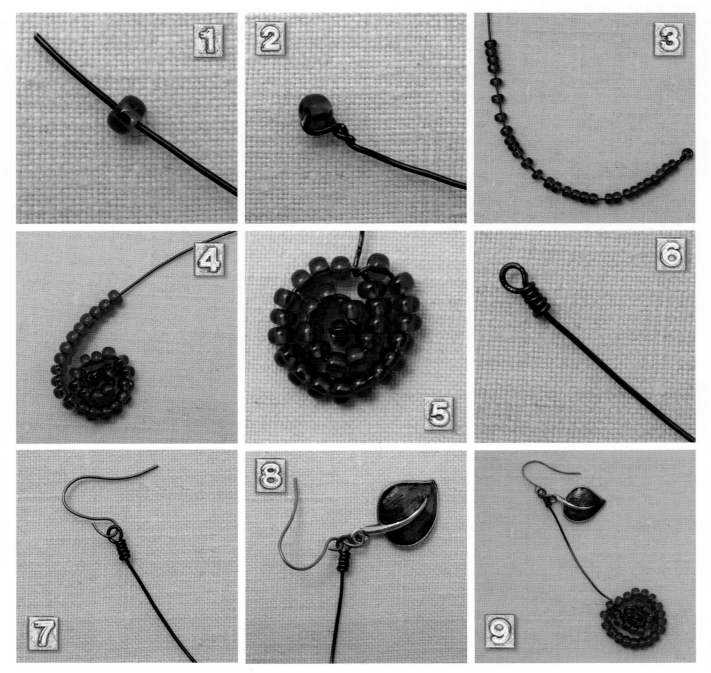

clusters

You can group beads in a different way to create clusters or bunches – these earrings are a perfect way to use this technique.

Everything you will need...

This technique lends itself to a whole variety of possibilities. As well as grapes, you could make blackberries or raspberries, or simply a mix of beads.

1. 2 silver open earring hooks with ball
2. 2 leaf charms
3. 24 links silver trace chain (12 links per earring)
4. 10 x ⁵/₁₆ (8mm) dark purple Swarovski glass pearls
5. 8 x ⁵/₁₆ (8mm) burgundy Swarovski glass pearls
6. 18 x 2in (50mm) silver headpins
7. 4 x ¹/₈in (3mm) silver jumprings
   round nose pliers
   snipe nose pliers
   side cutters

Assembling clusters

1 Open the loop on an earring hook, thread on 12 links of silver chain and close.

2 Thread a 2in (50mm) headpin through a glass pearl and make a hook, leaving the headpin length intact.

3 Pass the headpin length through the last link of chain.

4 Holding onto the top of the hook with snipe nose pliers, wrap the long end of the wire around itself a couple of times. This will create a small spiral of wire on top of the pearl. Cut off any excess headpin.

5 Repeat steps 2–4 until you have threaded 9 pearls (5 x dark purple and 4 x burgundy) randomly onto the length of chain.

6 Open a ⅛in (3mm) jumpring, thread a leaf onto it and close.

7 Open another ⅛in (3mm) jumpring, thread this through the loop on the earring hook and the jumpring holding the leaf, then close.

8 Finally, repeat the process to create the other earring.

VARIATION

THIS TECHNIQUE IS VERY SIMILAR TO MAKING THE GRAPES. THE DIFFERENCE IS THAT YOU CAN USE ANY SHAPED BEADS OR COLOURS YOU WANT. I LOVE PURPLES AND, USING THE GOLD LUSTRE AS INSPIRATION IN THE BIGGER DROPLET, I DECIDED TO USE GOLD CHAIN AND EARRING FITTINGS. THIS KEPT THE WHOLE DESIGN LOOKING REALLY WARM AND RICH.

The key to making these earrings look like bunches of grapes is to cluster more beads at the top of the chain and fewer at the bottom.

retro

These gorgeous pale colours have
given a 1950s feel to the design.

Everything you will need...

Using sieves is one of my favourite techniques; you can vary the design so much just by using different colours, shapes and sizes of bead.

1 2 sieves

2 2 x ⁵/₁₆ (8mm) flat back stud fittings

3 38 turquoise seed beads

4 2 x ¹/₄in (6mm) blue zircon crystals

5 12 x ¹/₄in (6mm) light azore crystals

6 24 x ¹/₄in (6mm) chrysolite crystals

7 ¹/₈₀in (0.3mm) nylon bead thread

glue

side cutters

retro

Assembling retro

PLANNING YOUR COLOURS CREATES STUNNING PATTERNS AND WILL SAVE A LOT OF TIME AND STRESS!

1 Tie a double or triple knot 2in (50mm) from one end of a 19³/₄in (50cm) length of nylon thread. Thread the long end of the nylon through the centre hole of the sieve and pull it all the way through, ensuring that the knot is against the concave surface.

2 Thread on the blue zircon crystal followed by a seed bead.

3 Next, thread the nylon end back through the crystal and down through the same hole. Pull both beads tight against the convex surface.

4 Thread the long nylon end into the next hole along. Repeat steps 2–3 using the light azore crystals to create a ring around the centre bead.

5 Now thread the nylon into the outer ring and repeat steps 2–4, this time using the chrysolite crystals.

6 When all the crystals have been used, push the nylon back through the last hole and tie this length to the 2in (50mm) of thread left at the central knot created in step 1. You can use a drop of glue to secure the knot.

7 Trim any loose ends. Glue a ⁵/₁₆in (8mm) flat back stud fitting onto the concave side of the beaded sieve slightly towards one edge of the sieve.

8 Finally, repeat the process to create the other earring.

If you use large beads you will not necessarily have space to use every hole.

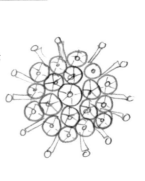

droplets

I always like a bit of
sparkle, so these sew-on
crystals are just the ticket.

Everything you will need...

Crystals come in a vast range of colours, shapes and sizes so the possible combinations are endless.

1. 2 x $^5/_{16}$ (8mm) flat back stud fittings
2. 2 x $^3/_{16}$in (5mm) silver jumprings
3. 2 x $^3/_{16}$in (5mm) gold jumprings
4. 2 x $^1/_2$in (12mm) silver sew-on crystals
5. 2 x $^3/_8$in (10mm) bronze sew-on crystals
6. 2 x $^3/_8$in (10mm) brown sew-on crystals

glue

snipe nose pliers

I GLUED THE TOP CRYSTAL ONTO A FLAT BACK STUD FITTING, BUT YOU COULD EASILY USE ANOTHER JUMPRING TO ATTACH IT TO AN EARRING HOOK INSTEAD.

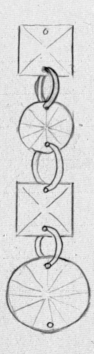

Assembling droplets

1 Glue a 5/16in (8mm) stud fitting to a 1/2in (12mm) silver sew-on crystal. Make sure that one of the holes of the crystal is not covered by the flat back of the stud.

2 Open a 3/16in (5mm) silver jumpring and link the 3/8in (10mm) bronze sew-on crystal to the 1/2in (12mm) silver one, then close.

3 Open the 3/16in (5mm) gold jumpring and use this to link the brown sew-on crystal to the other two crystals, and then close.

4 Finally, repeat the process to create the other earring.

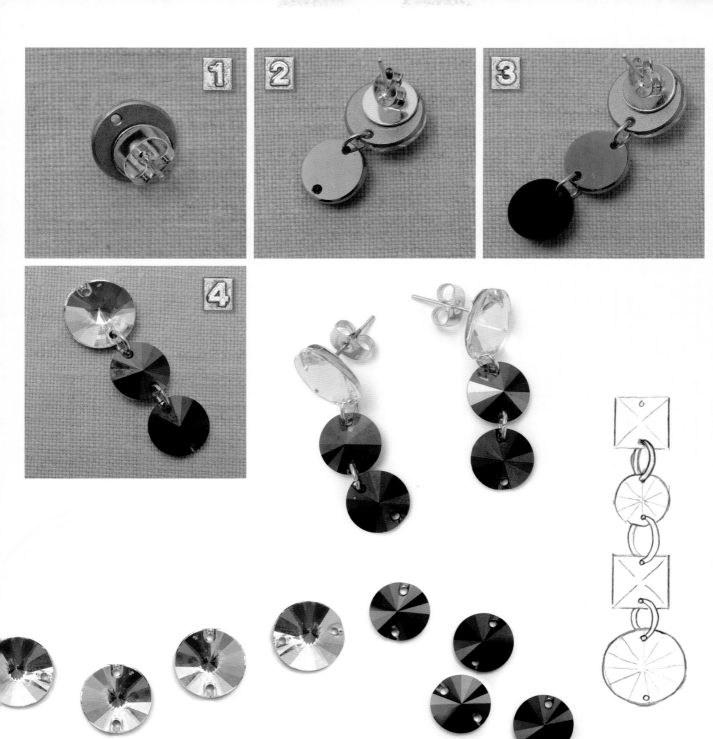

re-use

buttons

There is not much that can beat the fantastic variety of both antique and modern button shapes and colours.

Everything you will need...

When using recycled buttons you may struggle to find two exactly the same. Play on this idea in your designs.

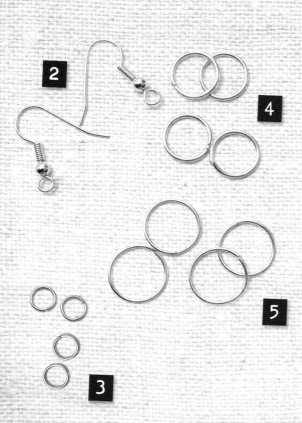

1 4 buttons

2 2 silver open earring hooks with ball

3 4 x $^9/_{32}$in (7mm) silver jumprings

4 4 x $^3/_8$in (10mm) silver jumprings

5 4 x $^1/_2$in (12mm) silver jumprings

snipe-nose pliers

flat-nose pliers

Assembling buttons

1 Open a $^3/_8$in (10mm) jumpring, thread it onto the left hole of the heart button and close.

2 Open another $^3/_8$in (10mm) jumpring, thread it onto the right hole of the same heart button and close.

3 Open a $^1/_2$in (12mm) jumpring, thread it through the left hole of the large round button and close.

4 Open a $^1/_2$in (12mm) jumpring, thread it through the right hole of the same button and close.

5 Open a $^9/_{32}$in (7mm) jumpring, link it through the two $^3/_8$in (10mm) jumprings at the top of the heart and through one of the $^1/_2$in (12mm) jumprings on the large round button, then close.

6 Open another $^9/_{32}$in (7mm) jumpring, link it through the other $^1/_2$in (12mm) jumpring on the large round button and through the eye loop on an earring hook and close.

7 Finally, repeat the process to create the other earring.

THIS DESIGN WILL LOOK FANTASTIC USING VINTAGE BUTTONS AND ANTIQUE SILVER CHAIN AND FINDINGS. WHY NOT GIVE IT A GO?

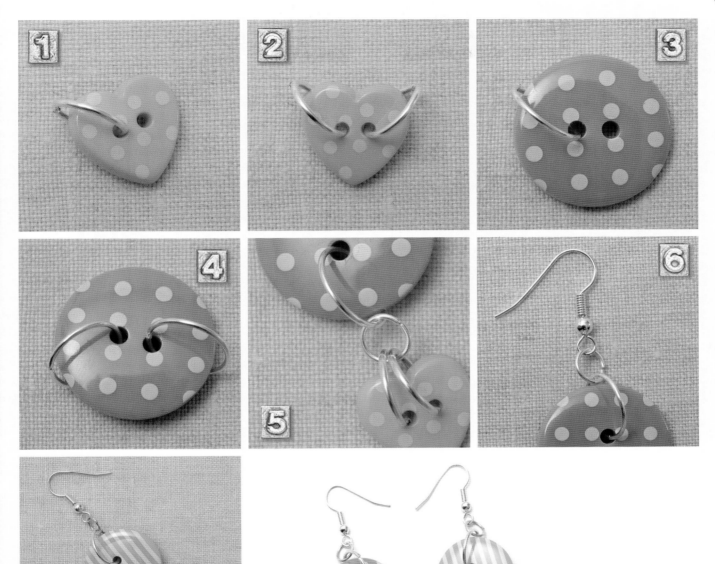

shoes

I came across a bag packed full
of miniature doll's shoes at a recent
secondhand sale and just had to have
them. This design is really about
being fun and funky!

Everything you will need...

Some shoes will be really easy to add a jumpring to, as they have ankle straps.

1 2 silver open earring hooks with ball

2 2 x $^3/_{16}$in (5mm) silver jumprings

3 2 x $^9/_{32}$in (7mm) silver jumprings

4 2 doll's shoes

Variation:

5 2 silver open earring hooks with ball

6 2 x 1$^3/_8$in (35mm) earring hoops

7 Selection of doll's shoes

snipe-nose pliers

flat-nose pliers

bradawl

shoes

Assembling shoes

1 If the shoes do not have a means to thread a jumpring onto them, hold the shoe firmly on a cutting mat (or chopping board), keeping your fingers away from the area to be pierced. Use the point of a small bradawl and twist backwards and forwards until you pierce through the plastic of the shoe.

2 Open a $^9/_{32}$in (7mm) jumpring, thread it through the hole in the shoe or around an ankle strap and close.

3 Open a $^3/_{16}$in (5mm) jumpring, link through the $^9/_{32}$in (7mm) jumpring and close.

4 Open the eye loop on an earring hook, then link to the $^1/_{16}$in (5mm) jumpring and close. Finally, repeat the process to create the other earring.

5 Alternatively, thread a selection of doll's shoes onto an open earring hoop and close. To finish, attach to the loop on an earring wire. Then repeat the process to create the other earring.

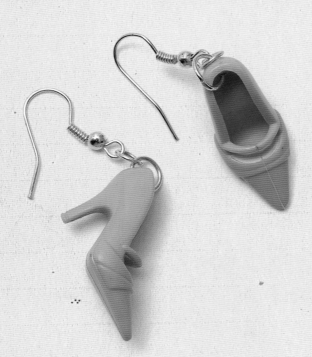

EMBRACE YOUR CREATIVE SIDE AND ENJOY MAKING SOMETHING UNIQUE TO CAPTURE EVERYONE'S ATTENTION.

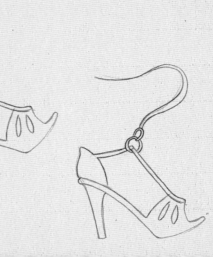

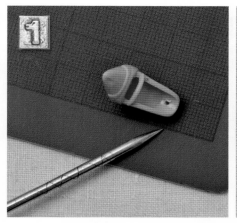

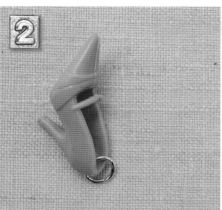

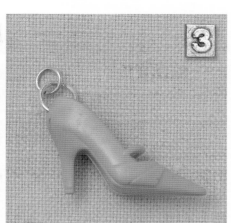

Variation

The plastic gives great colour, so be bold and add as many shoes as you can.

feathers

The wide variety of feathers available means you can create all sorts of looks. Why not go bohemian with these natural feathers?

Everything you need...

Choosing beads to complement your feathers will make your design subtle yet stunning.

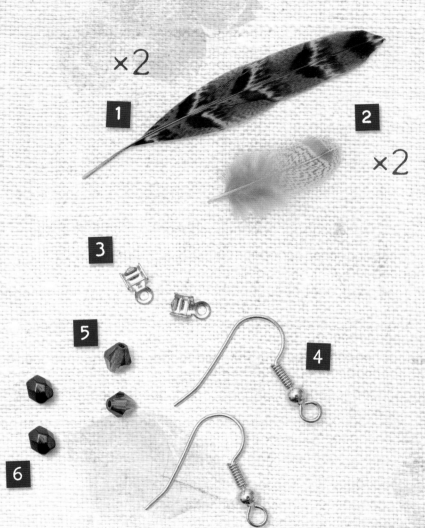

1. 2 large feathers
2. 2 small feathers
3. 2 gold ribbon crimps
4. 2 gold open earring hooks with ball
5. 2 x $^5/_{32}$in (4mm) smoked topaz Swarovski crystals
6. 2 brown beads

round nose pliers

flat nose pliers

snipe nose pliers

×2

×2

Assembling feathers

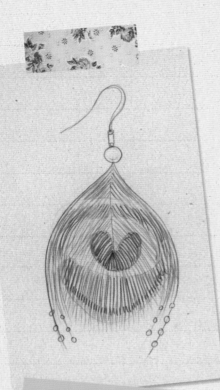

1 Holding a large found feather upright by the quill, pull any unwanted barbs downwards. These should peel away from the quill quite easily. Continue doing this until the feather is the size you require.

2 Cut the quill to the new length of feather, thread the cut end into the hole of a bead and out through the other side. Do this with as many feathers as you want, layering them to create different colours and textures.

3 Open a small ribbon crimp and fold the crimp over all the quills that are sticking out the end of the bead.

4 Using flat-nose pliers, squish the ribbon crimp tightly shut, then cut away any quills still sticking out of the top of the crimp.

5 Open the loop on an earring wire right out. Remove the small ball and replace it with a small crystal bead.

6 Re-form the earring hook loop using round-nose pliers and link onto the eyelet of the ribbon crimp then close.

7 Repeat the process to create the other earring.

PUSHING THE QUILL THROUGH A BEAD BEFORE ADDING A RIBBON CRIMP KEEPS THE FEATHER FACING THE RIGHT WAY.

Variation

Combining brightly coloured feathers with spotty beads can create a completely different look.

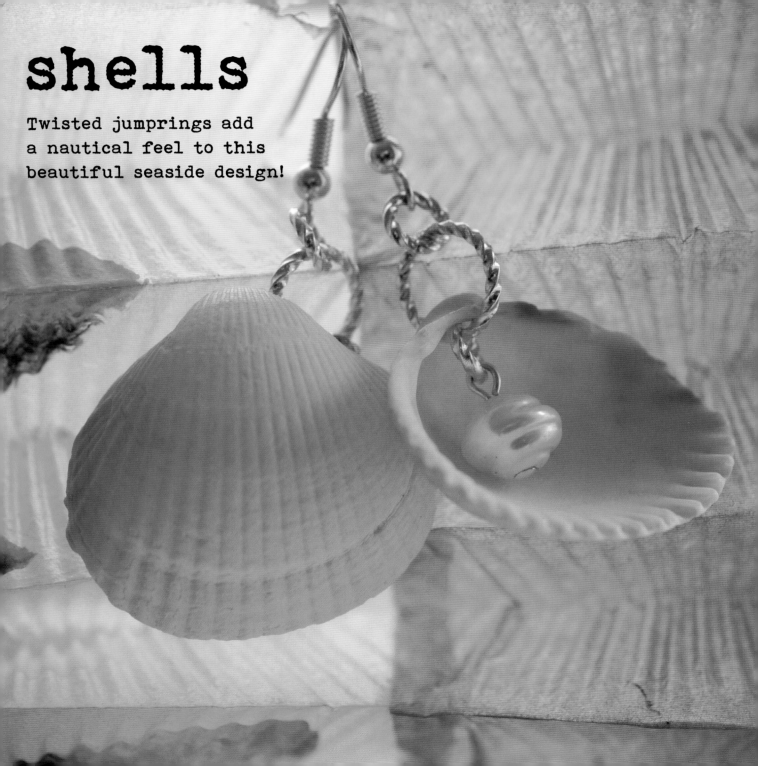

shells

Twisted jumprings add
a nautical feel to this
beautiful seaside design!

Everything you need...

Many of my happy childhood days were spent on a beach paddling in the shallows and collecting sea shells. In this design I've added pearls to create that special 'from under the sea' look!

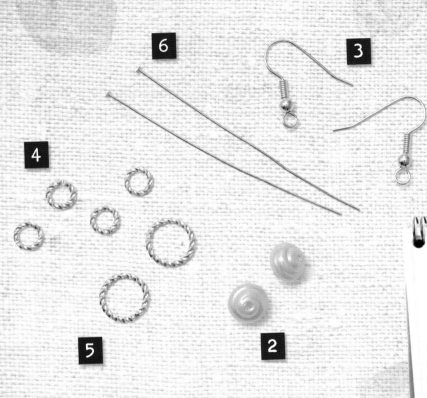

1. 2 shells
2. 2 pearls
3. 2 silver open earring hooks with ball
4. 4 x ¼in (6mm) silver twisted jumprings
5. 2 x ³⁄₈in (10mm) silver twisted jumprings
6. 2 x 2in (50mm) silver headpins

flat nose pliers

snipe nose pliers

side cutters

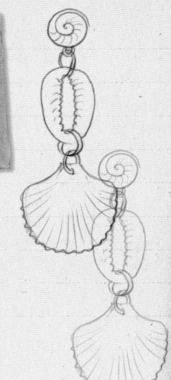

Variation

Using shells with a different shape and colour can create a completely new look.

Assembling shells

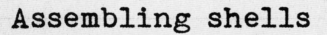

1 Open a ³/₈in (10mm) twisted jumpring, thread it through the hole in a shell and close.

2 Thread a 2in (50mm) headpin through a pearl (see basic techniques p23), then make an eye loop as close to the top of the bead as possible.

3 Open a ¹/₄in (6mm) jumpring, thread it through the eye loop at the top of the pearl and the ³/₈in (10mm) jumpring on the shell, and close.

4 Open another ¹/₄in (6mm) jumpring, thread it through the loop on an earring hook and the ³/₈in (10mm) jumpring, then close.

5 Finally, repeat the process to create the other earring.

IDEALLY, LOOK FOR SHELLS WITH HOLES IN THEM SO THAT THEY THREAD TOGETHER EASILY.

charms

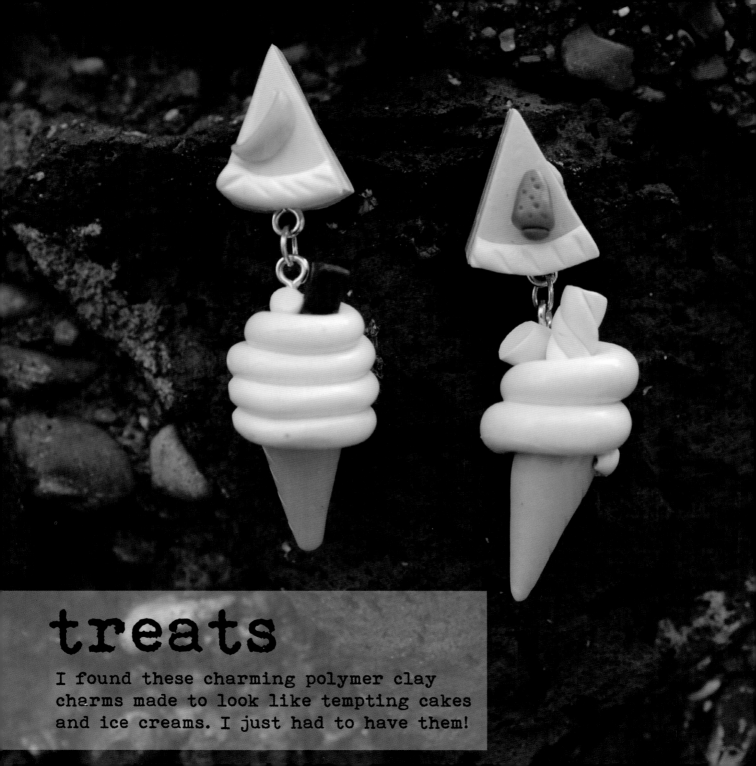

treats

I found these charming polymer clay charms made to look like tempting cakes and ice creams. I just had to have them!

Everything you will need...

I couldn't decide on what charms to buy, so I purchased one of each colour. They will still match because they are the same theme.

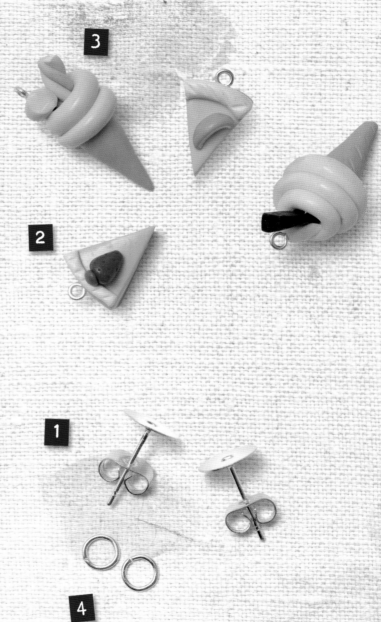

1. 2 flat back stud fittings
2. 2 cheesecake clay charms
3. 2 ice cream clay charms
4. 2 x ³/₁₆in (5mm) silver jumprings
   flat-nose pliers
   snipe-nose pliers
   glue

Clay charms can be quite heavy, so keep your designs simple.

Assembling treats

1 Glue a flat back stud fitting onto the back of a cheesecake charm as high up as possible.

2 Open a $3/16$in (5mm) jumpring and thread it through the eye loop of the ice cream charm.

3 Then thread the same $3/16$in (5mm) jumpring through the bottom eye loop of the cheesecake charm and close.

4 Finally, repeat the process to create the other earring.

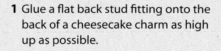

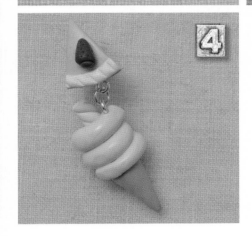

seaside

The fabulous colours of these
sea-themed lampwork shapes
inspired this project.

Everything you will need...

Just like the treats project, these beads are all different colours but will go together because of their theme.

1. 2 silver stud fittings with eye loops and scrolls
2. 2 x 2in (50mm) silver headpins
3. 4 x 2in (50mm) silver eyepins
4. 2 glass lampwork turtles
5. 2 glass lampwork fish
6. 2 glass lampwork starfish

   flat-nose pliers

   round-nose pliers

   side cutters

Assembling seaside

1 Thread a 2in (50mm) headpin through a turtle charm and form an eye loop as close to the top of its head as possible. Do not fully close the eye loop just yet.

2 Next, thread a 2in (50mm) eyepin through a fish charm and form an eye loop on the other side as close to the top of the fish as possible. Again, do not fully close this eye loop.

3 Using another 2in (50mm) eyepin, thread through the starfish charm and form an eye loop as close to the top of the starfish as possible. Fully close this eye loop.

4 Join the charms together by threading the top eye loop of the turtle onto the bottom closed eye loop of the fish and close.

5 Link all three elements together by threading the top eye loop of the fish onto the bottom closed eye loop of the starfish and close.

6 Open the loop on a stud post fitting, thread it through the top eye loop of the starfish and close.

7 Finally, repeat the process to create the other earring.

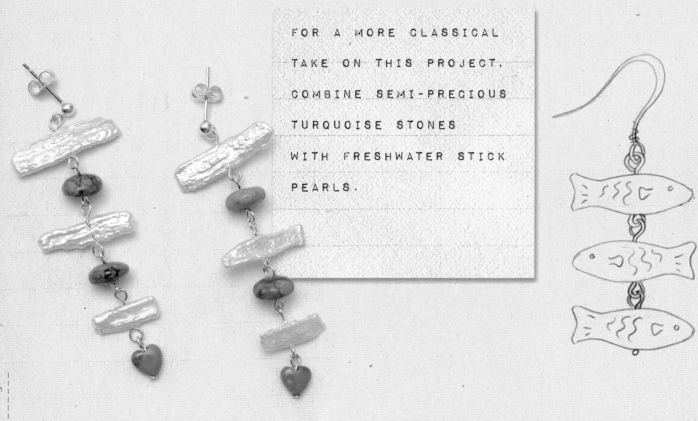

FOR A MORE CLASSICAL TAKE ON THIS PROJECT, COMBINE SEMI-PRECIOUS TURQUOISE STONES WITH FRESHWATER STICK PEARLS.

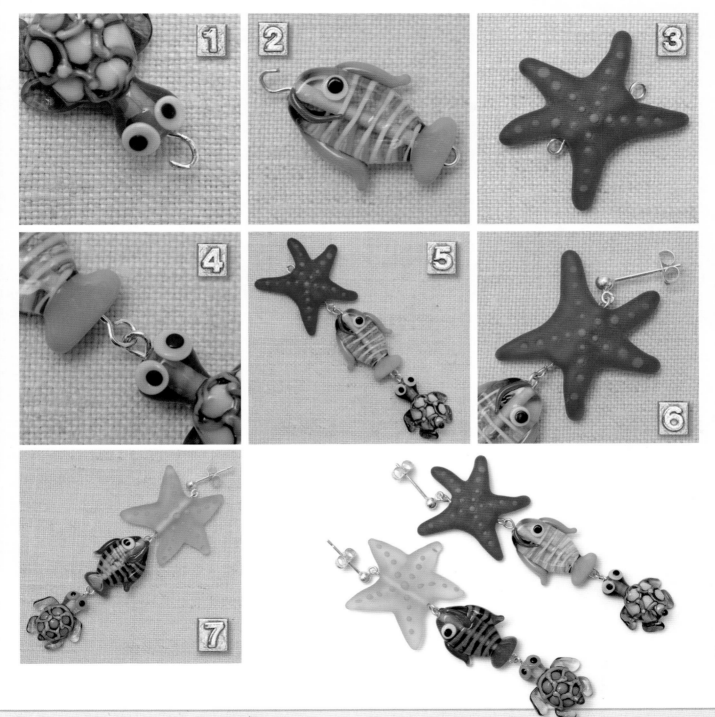

Everything you will need...

These metal charms are beautifully cast and have detail on both sides, so it doesn't matter if they spin round.

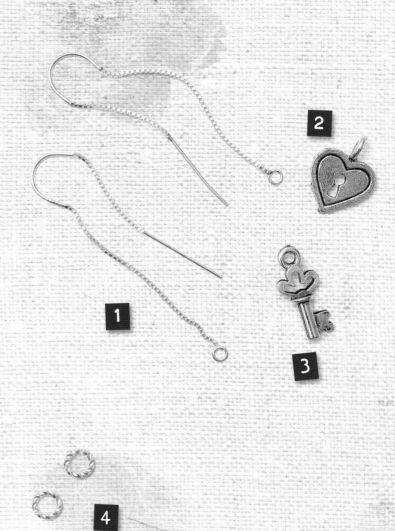

1 2 silver ear threads

2 1 heart lock charm

3 1 key charm

4 2 x ¼in (6mm) silver twisted jumprings

flat-nose pliers

snipe-nose pliers

Assembling secret

1 Open a ¼in (6mm) twisted jumpring.

2 Thread your heart lock charm onto the jumpring.

3 Link this twisted jumpring to the loop on the bottom of the ear thread and close.

4 Open another ¼in (6mm) twisted jumpring and this time thread the key charm onto it.

5 Link this jumpring onto the loop on the other ear thread and close.

WITH A DESIGN THIS SIMPLE, THE DETAILS ARE IMPORTANT. LOOK FOR TWISTED JUMPRINGS TO ADD THAT LITTLE BIT EXTRA.

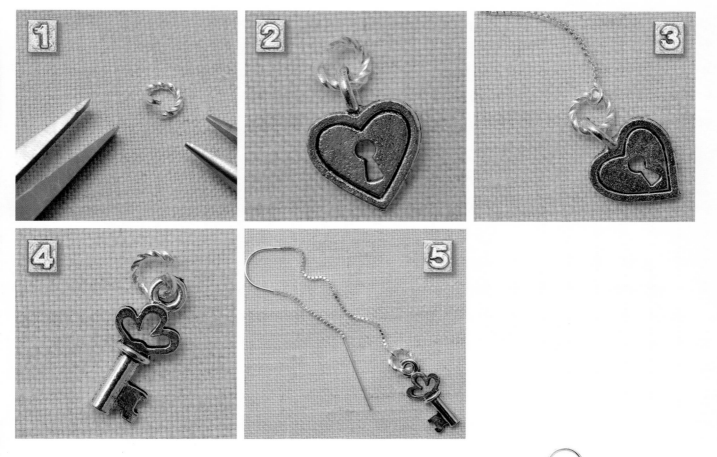

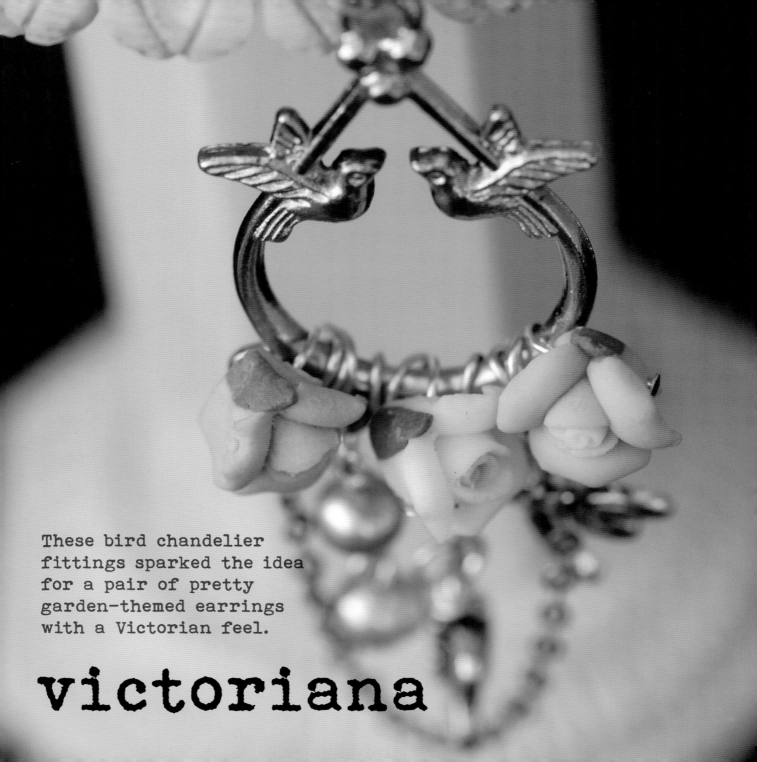

These bird chandelier
fittings sparked the idea
for a pair of pretty
garden-themed earrings
with a Victorian feel.

victoriana

Everything you will need...

Keeping the colours muted and using real freshwater pearls adds to the old-fashioned feel.

1. 2 antique silver open earring hooks
2. 2 bird-decorated chandeliers
3. 6 polymer clay roses
4. 2 dragonfly charms
5. 2 butterfly charms
6. 2 x ³/₁₆in (5mm) green pearls
7. 2 x ³/₁₆in (5mm) grey pearls
8. 12 x ³/₁₆in (5mm) silver jumprings
9. 4 x 2in (50mm) silver headpins
10. 2 x 2in (50mm) silver eyepins
11. 8 links silver trace chain
    (4 links per earring)
12. 76 links antique silver trace chain
    (38 links per earring)

flat-nose pliers
round-nose pliers
side cutters

victoriana

Assembling victoriana

1 Insert a 2in (50mm) headpin into a polymer clay rose and wrap the long end of the wire around the bottom of the chandelier fitting. Repeat this step using the two other flowers.

2 Open a $^3/_{16}$in (5mm) jumpring and thread it onto the antique silver chain (38 links long). Link it onto the left hoop on the chandelier fitting, then close. Take another jumpring and link this onto the bottom end of the chain and to the far right loop on the chandelier fitting.

3 Open a third jumpring, thread it through a dragonfly charm and the next loop on the chandelier fitting, then close.

4 Thread a 2in (50mm) headpin through a butterfly charm. Make an eye loop as close to the top of the butterfly as possible, then cut off any excess wire.

5 Open and thread another jumpring onto a length of silver chain (4 links long), link this to the top of the butterfly eye loop, then close. Link another open jumpring to the top of the small chain and to the middle loop on the chandelier fitting, then close.

6 Thread a 2in (50mm) headpin through a green pearl. Make an eye loop as close to the top of the pearl as possible.

7 Thread a 2in (50mm) eyepin through a grey pearl, and make an eye loop as close to the pearl as possible. Use this to link the green pearl, then close.

8 Open a final jumpring and thread it through the top eye loop of the grey pearl and the last remaining loop on the chandelier fitting.

9 Open the loop on an earring hook, link this to the chandelier fitting and close. Repeat the process to create the other earring.

IF DESIRED, CREATE THE SECOND
EARRING AS A MIRROR IMAGE,
CHANGING THE BEAD ORDER
TO ACHIEVE THIS.

inspirations

fig.2

The stunning Murano glass
and gold rococo architecture
I saw in Venice were the
inspiration for this project.

venice

Everything you will need...

These beads are so beautiful that I decided to use simple earring hooks to keep the focus on the beads rather than the findings.

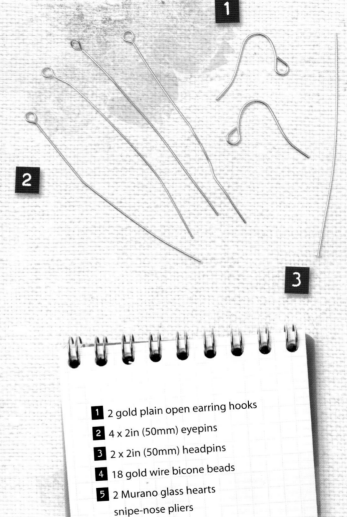

1. 2 gold plain open earring hooks
2. 4 x 2in (50mm) eyepins
3. 2 x 2in (50mm) headpins
4. 18 gold wire bicone beads
5. 2 Murano glass hearts
   snipe-nose pliers
   round-nose pliers
   side cutters

Assembling venice

1 Thread a 2in (50mm) eyepin through a Murano glass heart. Make an eye loop as close to the top of the heart as possible, but do not fully close it.

2 Thread a 2in (50mm) headpin through a small gold bead. Make an eye loop as close to the other end as possible, link it onto the eye loop at the bottom of the heart and close.

3 Thread eight small gold beads onto a 2in (50mm) eyepin and form a circle, keeping the beads as tight together as possible.

4 Wrap the remaining end of the 2in (50mm) eyepin around itself at the eye loop to secure the circle. Cut away any excess wire.

5 Connect this circle to the heart by threading the eye loop onto the loop at the top of the heart, then close.

6 Open the loop on an earring hook and thread on the circle of gold beads. Ensure that there are four beads on either side of the earring wire.

7 Finally, repeat the process to create the other earring.

WHEN YOU VISIT SOMEWHERE SPECIAL,
TRY AND FIND SOMETHING FROM THAT
PLACE TO USE IN YOUR DESIGNS TO MAKE
THEM REALLY MEMORABLE AND UNIQUE.

autumn

Autumn is my favourite season.
I love the rich earthy colours,
fresh misty mornings and
falling leaves.

Everything you will need...

Using copper-coloured findings really complements this design.

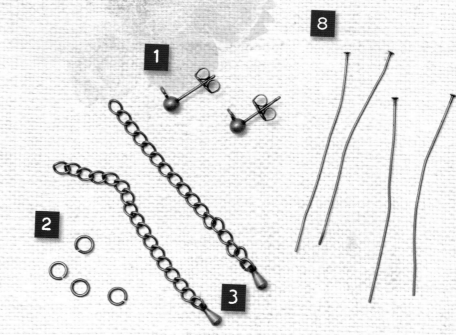

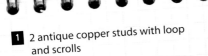

1. 2 antique copper studs with loop and scrolls
2. 4 x 3/16in (5mm) antique copper jumprings
3. 2 antique copper chain extenders
4. 2 antique copper leaves
5. 2 antique brass leaves
6. 2 metal charm beads
7. 2 large crystal beads
8. 4 antique copper headpins

   flat-nose pliers

   round-nose pliers

   side cutters

autumn

Assembling autumn

1 Thread a large copper leaf onto a ³/₁₆in (5mm) jumpring and close.

2 Open the loop of a stud fitting. Thread on the chain extender and the jumpring that's on the large copper leaf, and close.

3 Open another ³/₁₆in (5mm) jumpring and thread on the brass leaf.

4 Link this brass leaf onto the chain extender about halfway down and close.

5 Thread a headpin through the large crystal bead and form an eye loop as close to the top of the bead as possible. Join this bead by the eye loop to the extender chain halfway between the brass leaf and the bottom of the chain, then close.

6 Take another headpin, thread through a metal charm bead, and again form an eye loop at the top of the bead. Attach this to the top of the jumpring used for the large copper leaf and close.

7 Finally, repeat the process to create the other earring.

THINK ABOUT WHAT MAKES YOUR INSPIRATION TRULY SPECIAL AND LOOK FOR BEADS THAT CAPTURE THE VERY ESSENCE OF YOUR IDEA.

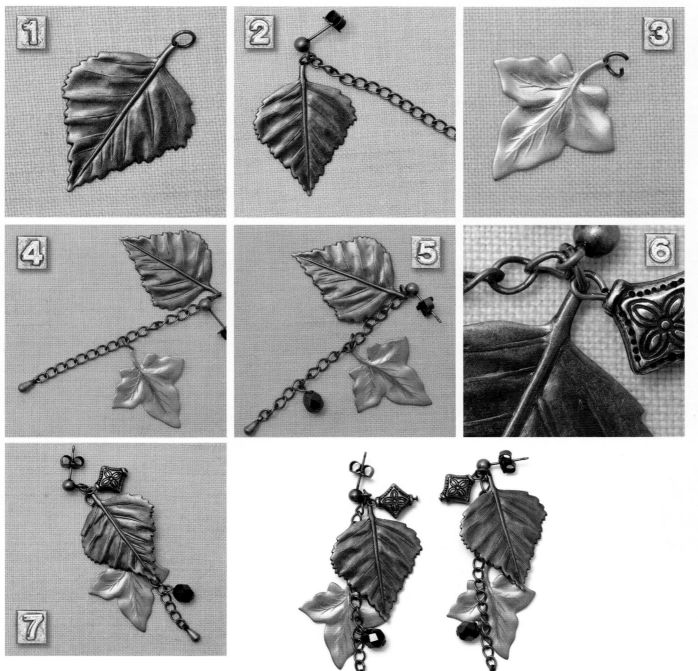

Bundled together, these chillies make a really striking design.

chillies

Everything you will need...

Anything can be an inspiration, from a colour to a place. Capturing your ideas on camera is a great way to store them.

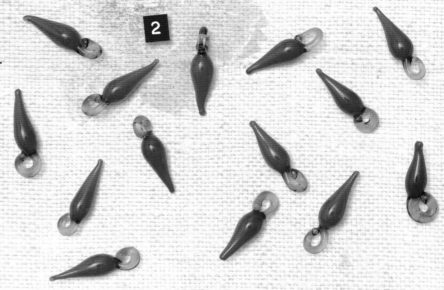

1 2 gold open earring hooks with ball

2 14 glass chillies

3 30 links gold trace chain (15 links per earring)

4 14 x ³/₁₆in (5mm) gold jumprings

snipe-nose pliers

flat-nose pliers

side cutters

chillies

Assembling chillies

1 Open the loop of an earring hook, thread on a length of chain, 15 links long, and close.

2 Link a ³/₁₆in (5mm) jumpring through the top of a chilli and the bottom link of the chain, then close.

3 Thread another ³/₁₆in (5mm) jumpring to another chilli and link this two links above the first chilli on the chain.

4 Repeat step 3 to add another chilli, but this time miss only one link out.

5 Continue to miss a link out each time until all the chillies have been added. Alternate the jumprings and chillies to the left- and right-hand sides of the links to ensure that the chillies are evenly spaced out.

6 Finally, repeat the process to create the other earring.

I TOOK THIS PHOTO ON MY
FIRST TRIP TO PORTUGAL,
AS I'D NEVER SEEN CHILLIES
BUNDLED UP IN THIS WAY. THE
COLOURS WERE SO INTENSE,
MUCH LIKE THEIR FLAVOUR!

chillies

sweets

Either you love liquorice
or hate it! I love it with
a passion!

Everything you will need...

Liking something so much is a great source of inspiration and starting point for any design.

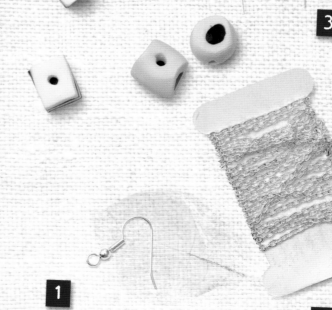

×2

1 2 silver open hook earring wires with ball

2 18 links silver trace chain (9 links per earring)

3 12 x 2in (50mm) silver headpins

4 12 polymer clay liquorice allsorts charms

flat-nose pliers

round-nose pliers

snipe-nose pliers

side cutters

sweets

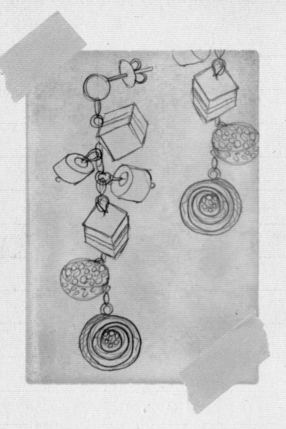

Assembling sweets

1 Thread a length of chain, nine links long, through the loop on an earring hook and close.

2 Thread a 2in (50mm) headpin through one of the polymer clay sweets and make a hook, making sure you leave the headpin length intact.

3 Pass the full length of the headpin through the last link of the chain. Holding the top of the hook with pliers, wrap the long end of wire around itself a couple of times to form a small spiral of wire on top of the sweet charm. Cut off any excess headpin.

4 Repeat steps 2–3 using the other five sweet beads and thread these randomly onto the rest of the chain.

5 Finally, repeat the process to create the other earring.

Earrings

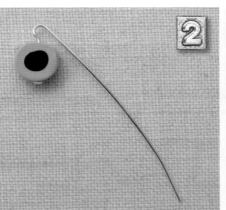

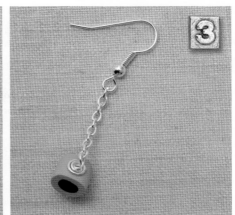

YOU COULD EASILY
HAVE A GO AT MAKING
YOUR OWN SWEETS
WITH MODELLING CLAY
AND CREATE A WHOLE
COLLECTION OF SOME
TANTALISING TREATS!

resources

Books

500 Earrings: New Directions in Contemporary Jewelry (Lark Jewelry) by Lark Books (Sterling, 2007)

All About Beads: Over 100 Jewellery Designs to Make and Wear by Barbara Case (David and Charles, 2006)

Beaded Earrings: A Beginner's Guide to Beadwork by Heather Kingsley-Heath and Susan Jane Bartucca (Useful Booklet Company, 2004)

Jewellery Making: A Complete Course for Beginners by Jinks McGrath (Apple, 2007)

The Earrings Book (Jewellery Handbooks) by Yvonne Kulagowski (A & C Black, 2007)

UK

Bead Aura
3 Neals Yard, Covent Garden
London WC2H 9DP
Tel: +44 (0) 207 836 3002
www.beadaura.co.uk

Beadworks UK Ltd
Trading as: *The Bead Shop*
21a Tower Street
London WC2H 9NS
Tel: +44 (0) 207 240 0931
www.beadshop.co.uk

Bijoux Beads
2 Abbey Street
Bath BA1 1NN
Tel: +44 (0) 1225 482024
www.bijouxbeads.co.uk

Cookson Precious Metals Ltd
59–83 Vittoria Street
Birmingham B1 3NZ
Tel: +44 (0) 845 100 1122
www.cooksongold.com

Jilly Beads
www.jillybeads.com

Palmer Metals
401 Broad Lane.
Coventry CV5 7AY
Tel: +44 (0) 845 644 9343
www.palmermetals.co.uk

Shiney Company
5 Saville Row
Bath BA1 2QP
Tel: +44 (0) 1225 332506
www.shineyrocks.co.uk

The Bead Shop Manchester
Office: 18 Upper Chorlton Road
Trafford
Manchester M16 7RN

Shop: Afflecks Palace
52 Church St
City Centre
Manchester M4 1PW
Tel: +44 (0) 161 232 7356
www.the-beadshop.co.uk

WORLDWIDE SUPPLIERS

www.adadornments.com

www.bedazzledbeads.com

www.gets.cn

www.landofodds.com

www.mkbeads.com

www.pandahall.com

about the author

Tansy Wilson successfully graduated from Brighton University with a BA Honours Degree in Three-Dimensional Design. This broad-based materials course enabled her to gain knowledge in a wide variety of materials which she still uses today within her own work. She also obtained a Post Graduate Certificate in Education and became a part-time lecturer working in several colleges and universities. She currently works for the University of the Arts London as an external moderator for Foundation Art and Design programmes as well as Drawing Awards and Certificates and at her local Further Education College teaching jewellery design. She has her own business making bespoke jewellery for private clients and also producing a craft range to sell at shows. She currently writes articles and creates jewellery projects for *Making Jewellery* magazine.

index

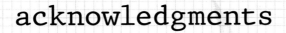

acknowledgments

I would like to say a massive thank you first to Toby, my lovely husband, who has often had to cook the supper as I am locked away in the workshop making a last-minute order. Also to my family and friends who have supported me through my career and tolerated numerous questions such as, 'do you like these beads?', or 'would these earrings look better in silver?'

I would like to say a special thank you to my friend Sian, whom I lived with as a student and now work with 20 years later!

Finally, I would like to say thank you to all the staff at GMC Publications for giving me the opportunity to write this book. Watching it evolve has been really exciting.

To place an order, or to request a catalogue, contact:

GMC Publications Ltd
Castle Place, 166 High Street, Lewes, East Sussex,
BN7 1XU
United Kingdom

Tel: +44 (0)1273 488005 Fax: +44 (0)1273 402866
Website: www.gmcbooks.com